Devi

Subhadra Sen Gupta has written over thirty books for children. Right now she is waiting for a time machine so that she can travel to the past and join Emperor Akbar for lunch. She loves to travel, flirt with cats and chat with autorickshaw drivers. If you want to discuss anything under the sun with her, email her at subhadrasg@gmail. com

Tapas Guha has been working for more than twenty years as an illustrator. He loves to draw comics and illustrate children's books. Ruskin Bond is one of his favourite authors and he loves Tintin comics.

Devi

SUBHADRA SEN GUPTA

Illustrated by

TAPAS GUHA

RED TURTLE
RUPA

Published in Red Turtle by
Rupa Publications India Pvt. Ltd 2017
7/16, Ansari Road, Daryaganj
New Delhi 110002

Sales centres:
Allahabad Bengaluru Chennai
Hyderabad Jaipur Kathmandu
Kolkata Mumbai

ISBN: 978-81-291-3654-1

First impression 2017

10 9 8 7 6 5 4 3 2 1

The moral right of the author has been asserted.

Printed by Nutech Print Services, New Delhi

CONTENTS

Parvati / 6

Daughter of the Mountains

Durga / 17

The Warrior Goddess

Saraswati / 30

A Goddess Loses Her Temper

PARVATI

Daughter of the Mountains

Himavat was the lord of the Himalayas and his wife was the heavenly nymph, the apsara Menaka. Parvati was their beloved daughter and she grew up into a gentle and very beautiful young woman.

Parvati led a happy, carefree life wandering in the hills and forests and bathing in the crystal waters of the

mountain streams and lakes. One day, while strolling on Mount Kailash, she came upon a young ascetic meditating under a tree. He was a very handsome young man even though his matted hair was tied in a knot on top of his head, his body was smeared with ash and he wore only a tiger skin.

This young sadhu was Lord Shiva, who is not just the god of destruction but also the Great Yogi, the greatest of all ascetics. And when Shiva is in the middle of his meditation, he does not like being disturbed at all.

Parvati promptly fell in love with him.

However, Shiva, sitting cross-legged with his eyes closed, concentrating on his mantras and prayers, did not even notice her. But Parvati could not stay away from Shiva and she began to come every day, bringing baskets of fresh fruits. She would fill his water pot with fresh river water, weave garlands and lay them at his feet.

Shiva calmly went on meditating and did not even open his eyes to see who was worshipping him every day.

Meanwhile, the gods were again having problems with the demons called asuras. This time it was with a demon called Taraka. Even though he often lost, Taraka kept on attacking them and Indra was getting really tired of fighting him. So the commander-in-chief of the army of gods went to Lord Brahma and asked for his help.

Brahma, the god of creation, was busy with his prayer beads and looked up in surprise, 'Ah, Lord Indra! What brings you here so early in the morning?'

Indra bowed low, 'My lord, as the wisest among the gods, you have to help me. Why is it that I can't kill Taraka? I often defeat him in a fight but he does not die,' Indra sighed, 'and then he comes back again!'

Brahma stroked his long white beard and said, 'I'm afraid Taraka will not die by your hand. We need a greater warrior to fight him.'

'Who?' Indra asked eagerly, 'Varuna? Surya? Agni? They are all ready to fight. Shall I call them?'

Brahma shook his head, 'No. They will fail too.' He thought for a while and said, 'If Shiva married Parvati, they would have a son who could kill Taraka.'

So now the gods also wanted Shiva and Parvati to marry but the problem was that Shiva did not even know she existed! How could he, when he wouldn't even open his eyes to look at her? What could Indra do?

When it came to the business of love and marriage, the expert was of course Kamadeva, the god of love. He carried a bow and arrow and the moment his arrow hit someone, the person would promptly fall in love. His famous bow was made with a branch of sugar cane, the bow string was a row of humming bees, and his arrows were tipped with jasmine, mango and lotus flowers. It was a true weapon of love.

So Indra went hurrying to Kama, who listened

and said, 'Hmmm...not an easy job, my friend. That young Shiva is a hard nut to crack. He does not flirt with apsaras, never chats with goddesses...all he is interested in is prayers and meditation.'

'But Parvati is so beautiful!' Lord Indra protested.

'How does that help when Shiva won't even open his eyes?' Kama asked.

'So what do we do? Give me an idea please!'

'I'll need the help of Vasanta, the god of spring. We have to make Shiva open his eyes and see Parvati, and Vasanta can help. Then I'll aim an arrow at him and he will fall madly in love.'

So Kama and Vasanta came to Kailash and though it was winter, Vasanta turned the mountainside into a spring landscape. The snow and cold winds vanished and a mellow breeze began to blow. The trees were suddenly covered with new green leaves and flowers bloomed everywhere as birds began to sing.

Then Kama hid behind a tree, all ready with his magical bow and arrow.

This sudden spring disturbed Shiva's meditation. Even though his eyes were closed, Shiva could feel the sudden change in the weather and he could smell the flowers and hear the humming of bees.

Parvati arrived just then and looked around in surprise. She laughed in delight seeing spring had arrived in the middle of winter in Kailash. She picked a handful of flowers and laid them before Shiva, and as she did so, her fingers touched his feet. Startled at hearing her laughter and then at her soft touch, Shiva opened his eyes and promptly Kama let his magical arrow fly.

Now the problem was that Shiva could be very bad-tempered. So when he woke from his trance and opened his eyes, instead of falling in love with Parvati, he was furious at being disturbed like this.

Instead of looking lovingly at Parvati, he glared around him and asked in a rage, 'Who has dared to disturb my meditation?'

When he spotted Kama lurking behind a tree, his third eye opened and a ray of fire shot out and burnt poor Kama to ashes. Then he closed his eyes and went back to his meditation.

Feeling very upset Parvati went home, and there she found Rati, Kama's wife, waiting for her, weeping at her husband being turned into ashes.

'Help me please, Devi Parvati!' Rati begged. 'Only you can persuade Shiva to bring my husband back to life. It was not Kamadeva's fault, you know. After all, he was only trying to help you.'

'I will save Lord Kama,' promised Parvati, with a fierce glint in her eyes, 'even if I have to die to do it. What Shiva did was very unfair and this time he will have to listen to me, even if that disturbs his meditation.'

A determined Parvati went into the forest and began to pray to Shiva asking for his help, and no one could stop her. As Shiva kept on ignoring her, she went on praying and performing the most difficult austerities.

In winter she stood in the waters of an icy stream; in summer she built four fires and sat in the middle and prayed on and on...

She hardly ate anything, living on just one leaf a day. And so she came to be called Aparna, or one who lives on leaves.

She became so thin and pale that her mother Menaka exclaimed in panic, 'O! Ma!' and Uma became one of the many names of Parvati.

Now the hills were full of sadhus and one day a young ascetic was going past where Parvati sat praying, and looked at her in surprise. He asked, 'Devi, why are you hurting yourself like this? What is it that you desire?'

'I want Shiva to marry me like the gods want him to. Also, he has to answer my prayers and bring Kama back to life. I will not give up till he listens to me.'

The ascetic laughed, 'Shiva? You are doing all this for that mad yogi? You are the daughter of Himavat, the lord of the Himalayas. You are so beautiful and talented. You can find someone much better than Shiva. He is not worth it, Devi.'

Parvati went on praying.

'He will make a bad husband,' the young ascetic continued. 'Even though he is a god he has no palaces and he will take you to live in a cave in Mount Kailash. He loves to wander around the hills and will forget to take care of you.'

'I know that,' nodded Parvati.

'He is not like Lord Vishnu,' the ascetic went on, 'all clad in golden silks and jewellery. He wears animal skins and smears his body with ash and his hair is matted and full of knots. How can you love such a mad man?'

'I know all that, but I still love him and I want to marry him,' Parvati said firmly and then she laughed. 'Perhaps I am mad too, like him.'

The ascetic gave a resigned sigh and said, 'Then, Devi Parvati, you win!'

As Parvati watched in surprise, the ascetic vanished and a smiling Shiva stood in front of her. He came up to her, took her hand and said gently, 'How could I not answer your prayers, my beautiful Parvati? Will you please marry me?'

Parvati said, 'I will marry you on one condition. You will first have to give back Kama's life.'

'Yes, I promise to do that.'

Parvati laughed, 'So Kama's arrow did have an effect?'

'Yes, it did,' said Shiva. 'I opened my eyes and saw the most beautiful goddess in the world!'

As all the gods celebrated, Himavat and Menaka held a magnificent feast to celebrate the marriage of their daughter. The gods showered flowers as Shiva and Parvati got married, and then went to live on Mount Kailash. And as he had promised, Shiva had given back Kamadeva his life, and Kama was there at the wedding with his wife Rati.

Soon Parvati and Shiva had a son named Kartikeya who became a fantastic warrior. He led the army of the gods against Taraka and killed the asura, establishing peace and happiness once again in heaven.

DURGA

The Warrior Goddess

The armies of the gods, or devas, and that of the demons, or asuras, were always at war. You would think they had nothing else to do. Lord Indra, the commander-in-chief of the army of the devas was always plotting to defeat the demons and conquer their cities. And the asuras were forever planning attacks against the devas to occupy Swarga, or heaven, the kingdom of the gods.

The king of the asuras was called Mahishasura, or Mahisha in short. He was very clever, and one day he came up with a clever plan that he was sure would defeat the devas forever. He went to a forest, sat down under a tree and began to pray to Lord Brahma, the god of creation. He hardly ate anything or drank any water; through the hottest summer and the coldest winter he did not move from his seat and prayed and prayed...

Brahma did hear his prayers but chose to ignore them. However, Mahisha refused to give up and prayed harder and harder. Years went by as Mahisha sat through storms and rain, snow and hot winds, praying on and on.

Now gods have to answer the prayers of the people who worship them, even demons. So finally Brahma very reluctantly came down to earth to see Mahisha and said, 'Here I am, Mahisha. Now why are you calling me?'

'Please, my lord,' said Mahisha very politely, 'will you grant me two boons?'

'Yes, I will,' sighed Brahma. 'How can I refuse? When people pray to me I always grant their requests, even those made by asuras. You know that. So what do you want from me?'

Then Mahishasura asked for two boons and they were very clever ones. First, he wanted the magical power to be able to change his body into that of any other living being—be it animal or human. That meant he could turn himself into a horse or a bird or a giant elephant. The second request was that he wanted to become the greatest of all warriors—one that no god, man or demon could ever defeat in battle.

Brahma was now in a fix! He knew immediately

what Mahisha was planning, but the problem was that he had promised this troublesome asura two boons and gods had to keep their word. The other gods protested loudly but poor Brahma was helpless. Very reluctantly he blessed Mahisha that no male—whether a god, man or animal—would be able to defeat him. And also that he would be able to change his form and turn into some other creature any time he wanted.

A triumphant Mahisha and his army of asuras promptly attacked Swarga. Indra and his army fought bravely, but because of Brahma's boon they were defeated. Finally, in desperation, they had to leave Swarga that was now occupied by the asuras. All the devas came down to earth and began to live disguised as ordinary people.

Now asuras are brave fighters but they have one problem—success often goes to their heads and they become cruel and proud. This is exactly what happened to Mahishasura, who thought he could do anything he pleased.

One day he was riding through a forest in Swarga and came upon the ashram, or hermitage, of sage Rishi Katyayana. The rishi lived in a thatched hut in the ashram and spent his days with his books and in peaceful meditation. Mahisha decided that this was an opportunity to trouble the sage and at the same time test his magical power to change his own shape.

So Mahisha changed his form into that of a woman, entered the ashram and began to destroy the rishi's garden, tearing up the flowers and breaking the branches of the trees. Then he stole the rishi's cows.

Now rishis were usually kind and gentle people but when they lost their temper, they could become very dangerous. They would begin to curse, and even the gods are afraid of the curses of rishis.

Now Mahisha thought he could get away without being cursed because he thought a rishi would not

curse a woman. But Rishi Katyayana had seen through his disguise!

The rishi's eyes became red with rage as he said, 'You have insulted me, Mahisha, though I had done nothing to harm you. So I curse you! You came here disguised as a woman, so it is a woman who will kill you one day. Brahma has said no man can kill you, but I say one day a woman will defeat and kill you!'

Mahishasura, drunk with power, just laughed.

Meanwhile the gods heard of Katyayana's curse and they hurried to meet the three most powerful gods—Brahma, the god of creation; Vishnu, the god of preservation and Shiva, the god of destruction.

Brahma, who was feeling rather guilty about the

boons, asked anxiously, 'But where can we find such a woman who can fight and defeat Mahisha?'

Vishnu, who is the cleverest among the gods, said thoughtfully, 'This cannot be any ordinary woman. We need a goddess and she has to be a great warrior who possesses all our energy and is better at battle than all of us.'

'There is no goddess like that,' Brahma said.

'Does that mean we have to create such a goddess?' Shiva asked, puzzled.

'How?' asked Lord Indra.

Then as all the gods looked at each other worriedly, Vishnu explained what they all had to do.

Accordingly, all the gods gathered at one place and began to concentrate hard till their shakti, or powers, began to flow out of them in golden streams and combined with each other to form the magnificent figure of a beautiful goddess.

Shiva named her the great goddess Durga, formed by the shakti or power of all the gods.

Shiva's shakti created her lovely face. Yama, the lord of death, gave her the dark cloudlike hair; and Vishnu, her ten hands to hold ten weapons. Chandra, the moon god; Varuna, the god of rain and Indra shaped her body. Brahma's power shaped her feet; Surya, the sun god, formed her toes and Agni, the fire god, opened her three lotus-shaped eyes. The third eye was at the centre of her forehead and Durga opened it only when she was angry.

Even the gods were dazzled by the power of this majestic goddess standing before them. She was radiantly beautiful, wearing shimmering silks and glittering jewels and her smile was kind and gentle.

Vishnu smiled back at her and said, 'Now, Devi Durga, you are our warrior goddess. So we have to arm you with some powerful weapons.'

Each god gave Durga a replica of his favourite weapon. She got Shiva's trident, the trishula, and Vishnu's discus, the sudarshana chakra. Varuna presented her with his conch shell to blow before battle and his noose, the pasha. Agni gave her his dart; Vayu, the god of the winds, his bow; and Surya, a quiver of golden arrows.

Indra gifted his famous thunderbolt, the vajra; and Kuber, the god of wealth, his mace, the gada. Kala, the lord of time, gave his sword and shield and

Vishwakarma, the architect of the gods, gave her his lethal battle axe. Finally Brahma put his string of rudraksha beads around her neck and Durga was ready for battle.

Durga said, 'I am pleased with the weapons, my lords, but I also need an animal I can ride in the battlefield and I need a fighting beast.'

Indra offered her his giant elephant Airavat; Vishnu wanted her to fly on his half-man-half-bird Garuda, but Durga chose the roaring lion of Himalaya, the lord of the mountains. As Durga stood before them armed with mighty weapons, her gigantic figure seemed to touch the sky.

And the gods decided happily that Durga looked very dangerous indeed!

Durga rode out to battle with her army of warrior goddesses, the Matrikas, and Mahisha could hear them coming from far away. Durga's lion was roaring angrily, the Matrikas were blowing on their conch shells and beating their battle drums, challenging the asuras to come and fight. Then Durga twanged the string of her giant bow and it sounded like a threatening roll of thunder.

Mahisha did not take the devis seriously and so first he sent out his asura army led by his generals Chiksura and Chamara. The fearsome demons came armed with swords, spears, hatchets and daggers, and a fierce battle followed between the Matrikas and the asuras. Spears whizzed through the air, swords clashed with loud clangs and the sky darkened with flying arrows. Pretty soon the goddesses began to win and the demons were being killed by the hundreds.

Realizing that they were losing, Chiksura and Chamara rushed to attack Durga together. They were sure they could defeat her. Chiksura showered Durga with arrows that she just swept away with a laugh. He pulled out a huge sword and Durga just swiped at it with her battle axe, and it broke into many pieces. Then she threw a spear that pierced his chest and killed him. Meanwhile, Durga's lion had come face-to-face with Chamara and killed the demon with his sharp claws.

An angry Mahishasura now came roaring in to face Durga and the world stood still to watch this mighty battle. Each time Durga attacked him, Mahisha would promptly change his shape and save himself.

He appeared as a lion and when Durga caught him in her noose, he became a giant holding a battle axe and slipped away. When the giant was speared, he changed into an elephant and came swaying towards Durga, trying to trample her to death.

The gods were all watching anxiously and they realized that Mahisha managed to always escape in the nick of time by changing his form. So Shiva came up to Durga and told her that Mahisha had to be killed at exactly the moment when he was changing into a new form because he was the weakest at that time. Durga's eyes blazed with anger as she took a few sips of the magical drink called Soma. She gathered all

her weapons together, and filled with the energy of the gods, she rode out for the final fight.

Mahisha faced her in the guise of a giant buffalo. He began to uproot trees with his pointed horns, breaking off rocks with his hooves and throwing them at Durga. She fearlessly jumped on the back of the buffalo and cut off its head with her sword. As she did so, Mahisha the demon began to appear from inside the animal's body but before he could change into something else, Durga aimed her trident at his chest and killed him.

With Mahisha dead, all the asuras panicked and ran away, and Durga rode back to Swarga in triumph as the delighted gods showered her with flowers. The heavenly nymphs, the apsaras, began to dance. The celestial musicians, the gandharvas, began to sing her praises. Then all the gods worshipped her, presenting her with precious jewels, gold and perfumes.

Devi Durga killed Mahishasura in autumn on the day celebrated as Dussehra. So even today we worship Durga, the magnificent warrior goddess, and her triumphant victory over Mahishasura, during the Durga Puja.

SARASWATI

A Goddess Loses Her Temper

Saraswati is the goddess of learning, speech and music, and she is also a sacred river like the Ganga and Yamuna. This beautiful, scholarly goddess, who is always dressed in white garments, likes to read and write books like the Vedas and play her veena—a stringed musical instrument. She looks like all the other goddesses—calm, smiling and gentle, but you should be a little careful around her. Because our Saraswati has quite a temper!

Saraswati was married to Brahma, the god of creation, and both of them flew around Swarga on their white swans, checking if everything was fine with the world and heavens that Brahma had created.

One day while Brahma was flying around as usual, he met a bad-tempered demon that attacked him with a sword. Now Brahma is a peaceful god and did not carry any weapons. He was only holding a lotus flower. So when the demon aimed his sword at him, Brahma swiped back with the lotus and, to his amazement, the demon fell down dead!

It so happened that when Brahma hit the demon, three petals of the lotus floated down to earth and landed in the desert where three silvery lakes, all filled with crystal clear water, sprang up. This place is called Pushkar because the petals had fallen from

Brahma's hand, and in Sanskrit 'pushp' means flower while 'kar' means hand.

Brahma was so very pleased at killing the demon that he decided to hold a yagya in celebration at Pushkar. A yagya is a religious ceremony where priests chant mantras before a holy fire. Then Brahma invited all the gods and goddesses to come to Pushkar for the

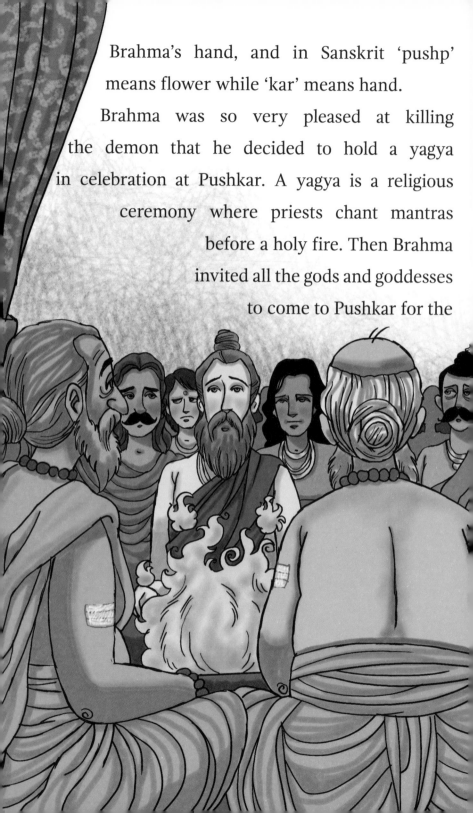

ceremony. Saraswati was very excited and was busy getting the place decorated with garlands of flowers. A feast of delicious dishes was prepared for the guests.

On the yagya day, the guests began to arrive one by one. First to come was Indra, the commander-in-chief of the army of the gods, and his wife Indrani. They came riding on his white elephant Airavat. Then Vishnu, god of preservation, and his wife Lakshmi flew in on his vehicle, the half-man-half-bird Garuda. Surya, the sun god, made a shining entrance driving his golden chariot that was drawn by seven white horses. Shiva, the god of destruction, dressed in his tiger skin, strolled in with his wife Parvati and his pet bull Nandi.

Saraswati was delighted to find that everyone had accepted her invitation. This was going to be a great ceremony! She rushed inside to get ready.

A yagya is always celebrated together by a husband and wife. So Brahma and Saraswati had to sit side by side before the sacred fire as the priests chanted the holy mantras, offering ghee, flowers and sandalwood to the fire. Soon the guests had gathered all around to watch the ceremony. Brahma sat waiting beside the fire, but Saraswati had still not arrived.

Brahma turned to Indra and said, 'Lord Indra, would you please go and find my wife. It is the sacred hour and the yagya has to start soon...'

Indra went in and found that Saraswati was still getting ready, so he said, 'Lord Brahma waits for you before the fire, Devi Saraswati.'

'What's the hurry, my lord?' asked Saraswati, as one maid combed her hair and another was busy drawing pretty patterns on her hands and feet. 'After all, today is a very special day and I want to look my best. Tell my lord Brahma to be a little patient.'

Indra came back and gave Saraswati's message to Brahma, who gave a patient sigh. Then everyone waited and waited. And waited...

A bored Shiva closed his eyes, and touching his rudraksha beads, began to meditate. Vishnu began to chat with Lakshmi and Parvati. Indra tried to hide a yawn and Surya seemed to have fallen asleep.

Then the priest whispered nervously to Brahma, 'My lord, the sacred hour is going by. Devi Saraswati has to come soon or it will be too late to start the yagya!'

So poor Indra was sent inside again and found Saraswati sitting before all her jewellery, trying them on one by one, as the goddess simply could not make up her mind what she should wear.

'Please, Devi,' Indra said urgently,

'everyone has been waiting for so long. Aren't you ready yet?'

'Oh, I am coming!' Saraswati said irritated. 'Can't you all wait for a little while longer?'

'Devi, the sacred hour is passing, the priests are getting anxious... if it is too late we will miss the sacred hour and then we'll have to postpone the yagya.'

Then Saraswati lost her temper. 'Oh you fools!' she stamped her foot, 'I am the goddess of learning and I wrote the sacred books of the Vedas. Are those priests trying to teach me the rites of the yagya?'

So with a sad sigh Indra came back and gave Saraswati's message to Brahma, and then everyone waited again.

Finally Brahma turned to the priest and asked, 'Can't we start without Devi Saraswati?'

'No, my lord!' the priest said in panic. 'No yagya can start without the wife as it would bring bad luck.'

'I've had enough!' said Brahma angrily. 'I am the god of creation and I will not wait any longer!' Then he turned to Vishnu and said, 'Go and find me another wife. I am not waiting any longer for Saraswati.'

So Vishnu and Indra hurried out to find a bride

for Brahma, and in a nearby field they found a pretty girl named Gayatri. She was a farmer's daughter, herding her cows. They brought Gayatri and her family to the yagya place and Brahma quickly married her. So, with a new wife beside him, the yagya began.

When Saraswati finally arrived, she found a strange woman sitting beside her husband and they were performing the rites of the yagya together. She frowned and asked Vishnu, 'My lord, who is this woman sitting in my place before the fire?'

'Ummm...well...actually, my lady,' Vishnu began apologetically, 'as you were so late, Lord Brahma has taken a new wife.'

'A NEW WIFE!!' Saraswati's eyes blazed with anger, 'I am his wife. How dare he do this without my permission?'

'But Devi, I went to call you twice and...' Indra mumbled trying to explain. 'The sacred hour was passing and the priests insisted that there should be a wife present...so Lord Vishnu and I found Gayatri and...'

Saraswati was furious and glared at Brahma, 'Couldn't you be a little patient on this important day?' Then she turned to Indra and Vishnu, 'And you two! The moment he asked you to find a wife you went rushing off to obey? Never thinking how that would hurt me?'

'We had to obey, Devi...' Indra began to explain.

'No, you did not! How did you all forget that I am the goddess of speech and whatever I say will come true?'

The entire gathering of gods and goddesses went silent with dread as everyone waited to see what Saraswati would do next.

She took a deep breath and said, 'I, Saraswati, sacred goddess of speech and learning, mother of the Vedas, I curse you!' And as everyone held their breath, she let the terrible curses fly.

Saraswati first turned to Brahma and said, 'You, my lord, do not think of my feelings at all and so you will be a forgotten god. No one will worship you anywhere after today. Vishnu and Shiva will be far more popular. There would be no temple built to you anywhere, except the one here at Pushkar. And there would be no festivals celebrated in your name.'

Then she turned to Lord Vishnu, 'And you, Lord

Vishnu... you will be born on earth as a man and as you have insulted me today, your wife too will be insulted by another man.'

By then Indra had turned pale with fear as Saraswati said, 'You, my lord, came twice to call me but did not bother to warn me that my husband was about to take another wife. Why should you? Because you think I am just a goddess. So, one day you will be defeated and driven out of heaven and you will have to beg a goddess to save you.'

Then Saraswati marched up to the yagya

altar, sat down on the other side of Brahma and he completed the ceremony with two wives beside him.

All of Saraswati's curses came true. Today, in India there is only one temple where Brahma is worshipped and that is at the temple at Pushkar, which is a place in Rajasthan. Pushkar has three lakes where the lotus petals fell from Brahma's hand. The Brahma temple is a small temple on a hill beside the largest lake.

Vishnu came to earth in the avatar or re-incarnation of Lord Rama. His wife Sita was kidnapped and insulted by Ravana, the demon king of Lanka, just as Saraswati had cursed.

As for poor Indra, he was defeated by the demon Mahishasura and had to escape from Swarga. He would get his kingdom back only after another goddess, the warrior Durga, defeated and killed Mahisha.

Today, if you visit Pushkar, you can see the three lakes and also find two temples where the two goddesses Saraswati and Gayatri are worshipped. Here Saraswati is often called Savitri and the two temples to Savitri and Gayatri stand at two ends of the town. Maybe that is to make sure that the two goddesses don't meet and start another battle of curses!